A POETICS OF HIROSHIMA

Also by William Heyen

A POETICS OF HIROSHIMA

& Other Poems

by
William Heyen

etruscan press

Etruscan Press
Wilkes University
84 West South Street
Wilkes-Barre, PA 18702
www.etruscanpress.org

10 9 8 7 6 5 4 3 2 1

Publishers Cataloging-in-Publication
(Provided by Quality Books, Inc.)

Heyen, William, 1940-
    A poetics of Hiroshima / William Heyen. ~ 1st ed.
    p. cm.
    ISBN-13: 978-0-9797450-5-8
    ISBN-10: 0-9797450-5-5

    1. Holocaust, Jewish (1939-1945)~Poetry.
    2. American poetry~21st century.   I. Title.

PS3558.E85P64 2008   811'.54
           QBI08-600245

Cover Art:
The three superimposed single-line drawings of William Heyen are by
Holocaust survivor and artist Alfred van Loen.

Cover and Interior Design by Nicole DePolo

Etruscan Press is committed to sustainability and environmental stewardship.
We elected to print this title through Bookmobile on FSC paper that contains
30% post consumer fiber manufactured using biogas energy and 100% wind
power.

Acknowledgments

Grateful acknowledgments to the editors of the publications in which many of these poems and prose pieces first appeared: *American Poetry Review* ("Sunlight"); *Artful Dodge* ("Iwo Dahlia"); *Chautauqua* ("Sleepers," "The Sea"); *The Darfur Anthology* [Elgin, IL: Elgin Community College, 2007] ("The Plugs"); *English Record* (the prose piece "History," "The Pearl Museum"); *Great River Review* ("A Poetics of Hiroshima," "Directive"); *Hotel Amerika* ("The Carriages"); *Margie* ("Museum Visitor Coda"); *North Stone Review* ("Beauty"); *The Ohio Review* ("The Streetcar: August 6, 1945"); *River Teeth* ("Lullaby"); *The Seventh Quarry* [Swansea, Wales] ("Poetry," "Anthem"); *The Southern Review* (the poem "History," "To Janusz Korczak," "Dr. Heim," "Two Young Men," "Autumn Rain, 1946," "Rose"); *Tar River Poetry* ("Judgment").

"A Poetics of Hiroshima" was reprinted in *The Seventh Quarry*, "Sleepers" in *Poetry Kanto* (Japan). "The Streetcar: August 6, 1945" was reprinted in *The Pushcart Prize XXV* (2001) and in the author's *The Confessions of Doc Williams & Other Poems* (Etruscan Press, 2006).

For Mihaela Moscaliuc & Michael Waters

Contents

A Poetics of Hiroshima

I

Sunlight

It Came to Pass

that Josef Mengele realized,
as he stood at his station
conducting destiny with his baton,
that he himself was demon, son
of the scion of morning. He ordered
a cessation to the gassings....

No, he did not. This was merely
a story that began to form in me,
in us, as though a new gospel
were possible, crematory skies
retroactive, bodies returned
to living beings. Tell me a story,

a poet asked, tell me a story.
We did. We had hope for the dead,
but Mengele, now, resumes
forming sounds with his baton,
one story after another, theirs,
but his, & his, & his.

Ghost Story, 1944

Then it was spring at Birkenau. Cousins Dario & Morris
raised their hands, said they were barbers. Then
they were taken to a brick building, given shearing scissors,
led to a room packed tight with dead women. Then
their Kapo guard jumped up on the naked bodies,
boots & all. Then he demonstrated. Then

it was the cousins' turn. Then they moved too slowly.
Then the Kapo caned them. Then they sheared wildly until
one stepped on a stomach, this forced gas through the mouth,
she groaned, she near scared them to death.
Then they learned their work, then came to witness
the mass gassings.... Decades later Morris testified,

"When they opened the door, I see these people....
I see them all standing up, some black and blue from the gas.
No place where to go. Dead. If I close my eyes,
the only thing I see is standing up, women with children
in their hands." Then for the rest of his life Morris heard
voices in his head calling out "God, God."

The Pearl Museum

Included in transports from the extermination camp at Treblinka in Poland to SS headquarters in Berlin between October 1942 & August 1943, last on a roster of plunder signed (no doubt proudly, patriotically) by Commandant Franz Paul Stangl, were several thousand strings of pearls.

I know nothing of pearls in those days—just where they came from, how they were strung, how fashionable they were, how common or uncommon they were. Were some already cultured, grown from seed in tanks or roped-off seabeds? Were some already resin or plastic? Or were all still formed naturally in oysters' flesh as the bivalves coated grains of sand or bits of other intrusive foreign matter to render them harmless?

The Treblinka horde must have been of various quality & therefore of various worth to the Reich. They were a young girl's birthday gift; they were great-grandmother's heirloom string, lustrous for a hundred years, the silver-gray flawless beauties graduating in size toward the largest, pendant at center, & away. We don't know if the thousands of strings of pearls were classified by Stangl's jewelers, each placed in its own envelope or pouch, but, surely, they did not reach Berlin tangled like nacreous worms in a crate.

I would like to know what happened to the Jews' pearls when they reached the capital of the Reich, when they reached SS headquarters on *Prinz Albrecht Strasse*. Since only about 60 of 1,000,000 prisoners survived Treblinka, & since Stangl's list specified the far-from-precise "several thousand," did many strings that would not be missed go home that very evening to flatter the necks of beloved SS wives & daughters? In any case, most of the pearls must still be extant—one string in a safe deposit box in Rome or Lisbon or Zurich, another among a wealthy German woman's jewels in Hildesheim, a third at this very moment for sale in a shop in Montreal, another on display

4

in a Manhattan window, a fifth ...

It could be that particularly rare pearls were removed from strings for fascist redeployment in other rings, tiaras, necklaces. For the sake of their & our & the victims' souls, I would like the German people to make a census of these pearls, to trace each string & each separate pearl from time of seizure at Treblinka to its current whereabouts. I would like these pearls to be collected. I would like us to visit them in their own museum in Berlin or Jerusalem, these *Shoah* syllables, tier after tier of them in arks in dimly-lit sacristies where we could remember them even with our eyes closed, where we could listen to them all night long.

Sleepers

The child dies. The father
hires an old man to say prayers
over the body before burial.

The father falls asleep, dreams
his child tugs at his sleeve,
Father, I'm burning,

can't you see I'm burning?
He awakens to find
the old man asleep, & a candle

searing the arm of the corpse....
This dream was told to Freud,
decades before the Holocaust....

    Have we fallen asleep while praying?
    We enter the father. We suffer him
    suffering that cry,

        Father, I'm burning, can't you see
        I'm burning? He awakens
        to find us asleep & a candle

        sputtering in his child's arm.
        We try to extinguish it—
        no use. We cover the candle

        with sackcloth, but the candle burns.
        This, now, is our tableau,
        we sleepers who cannot awaken....

        The only movement now is candleflame
        under our closed lids.
        We are the wick, that corpse our wax.

Lullaby

A dream last night. Adream last night, I was standing behind a tall SS man who was drowning a newborn Jewish baby under a faucet. He was singing. I couldn't make out his words, not above the rushing water, but I knew what they were. He was singing, "Here you go, little Moses, down the stream." I knew these words because in my waking life I'd read them in a survivor's testimony in Henry Greenspan's *On Listening to Holocaust Survivors: Recounting and Life History.* The child had been born in another room just minutes before. Carrying it, a tall SS man entered where the survivor-witness was sweeping, held it upside down under a tap, turned on the water, & sang as though singing a lullaby as he drowned this baby—"Here you go, little Moses, down the stream."

I believe I was not that SS man in my dream. I saw his whole body from behind, was not fused with him—unless of course my memory of my dream censors it & makes it bearable for me; unless of course these perceived divisions between & among dream-personae are illusory. But, in any case, it did not occur to me in this dream to interfere, either, to try to save the baby. In my powerlessness as a reader of history, it may be, I had projected myself into the helpless witness that the survivor had been.

In Greenspan's book the witness did not say he had not seen that SS face, but I could not see it in my dream. The SS man's back was to me as he bent over the sink. I'm not sure I could see the child as he held it upside down under the water, but maybe, for just a moment, a durational traumatic moment that would abide in me, I did see the baby, right through that SS body, saw one of my own four grandchildren. At one time or another I would sing to each of these children, "You are my sunshine, my only sunshine," a lullaby that always moves me. "I bowed my head and cried." But my grandchild would be with me there when I finished that song.

Apparently the survivor did not know the name of that SS murderer. Maybe he was a doctor, maybe an orderly of some kind or an officer passing through. He must have enjoyed what he was doing, & enjoyed his own obscene wit. Was he singing to himself, or to the sweeper? His song addresses the baby—"Here you go...." The SS man, the sadistic brainwashed brute, holds the newborn by its feet under the water—this happened to happen not in Auschwitz but in Hamburg—& sings to it as he fills its nostrils & mouth & extinguishes it.

I have read a hundred Holocaust books, seen films, heard survivors speak in person & on tape, have immersed myself in that history, have had many nightmares over the decades as I've visited, only *visited*, atrocity. In all senses, I am shadowed for the rest of my days. I knew & felt this baby's death before, but this is now again the first death after which there is no other, no worst there is none. The beast of my own German blood holds the newborn upside down under the running water & sings, "Here you go, little Moses, down the stream."

Dr. Heim

In less than a year after / being assigned to Mauthausen /
our Dr. Heim operated / on 540 prisoners, / amputated /
healthy limbs, / cut & left abdomens / unsutured /
to observe infection / & agonized death. /

One day he selected / two young men for their /
complete sets of teeth. / He himself injected them /
with poison, / then / decapitated / them /
ordered their heads / boiled & cleaned. / Dr. Heim /

displayed one skull / on his desk, / gifted / a like-minded /
colleague with the second.... // After the war /
we find him / in Mannheim / in gynecology.... //
Then he & his wife move to Baden-Baden to open

a practice.... / Evidence / of his war crimes /
surfaces.... // He escapes to Argentina for /
the remainder / of his works & days. // ... What do I, /
for one, desire / to make of our Dr. Heim? / Need I /

know more, / or is outline / sufficient for me, / a German
doctor as exemplar, / the biblical / "mystery of iniquity"? / ...
He enjoyed / fishing mountain streams, / attending to /
reveries / of his Reich even / while holding a trout before /

releasing it, admiring its rainbow / shimmer / from /
gills to tail / as though / it were— / this very /
home here, / his name, / this poem— / what I & he /
had always, / somehow, / wished / & worked for.

Poetry

I don't know the Lithuanian national anthem,
but know that at Kaunas in 1941 a murderer
climbed atop Jews' bodies with his accordian.
To hear him brought tears to patriots' eyes.

He is bloody from his work, but picture him,
& listen as the anthem swells. His wrists oscillate,
his instrument praises & swears allegiance,
many hum or sing along, his chords vibrate....

Who am I kidding? You nor I can see or hear him,
nor can the dead though poetry would have it so,
if you know what I mean, which I sometimes do.
Kaunas recedes with the chords of that anthem.

All we hear *ad nauseum* is that history matters,
that we'll learn it or repeat it as the years
reveal our primal human face. Picture
the onlookers, their throats tight for their nation,

while one who clubbed innocents to death
squeezes air from those bellows, then
pulls his hands apart to draw air in again.
Take deep breaths with me, then try holding one.

The Word

I'll give you a hint: it rhymes with lice.
First, this:

Laurence Rees in his *Auschwitz: A New History* mentions
interviewing Wilfred von Oven,

once Josef Goebbels' personal attaché,
in 1990 a gray,

elegant, sophisticated man. Eventually, over tea,
Rees asked him if he

could sum up his experience of the Third Reich
in one word, what would it be?

"Well," Herr von Oven said, "if I had to summarize
my experience in one word,

"that word would be ... *paradise*."

Anthem

As that murderer at Kaunas pulls his hands apart
to draw air into his accordian's bellows,
he seems to welcome us as though for an embrace.
Nor do his wrists pull straight sideways, but oscillate,

here, I'll show you, though this time I am not the one
who just a few minutes ago swung a club
that pounded innocent people to death. Like this, though,
my sinewy, muscular music swells, do you hear it?

For us, I grant us, that episode sounds very far away.
As I write, the sympathizers who heard that brute
play their anthem in triumph atop the victims
are themselves nearly dead, or dead, as dead

as poetry might allow the guilty ever to be, ...
for here is our anthem now, played above them,
rupturing their graves to attempt to remind them
how their hearts filled with gratitude that day.

Exercise

& consider Ernst Krankemann, German criminal,
sent from Sachsenhausen to Auschwitz
to serve as Kapo,

1940. Krankemann, so fat he could hardly walk, squatted
on top of a giant roller used to shape
the square at camp's center.

Twenty or twenty-five workers were hardly able to pull it.
Krankemann, above them, whipped them—
"Faster, you dogs."

One evening, a prisoner collapsed & could not rise.
The fat Kapo ordered the others
to pull the roller

over the exhausted one, & they did, & heard what they heard.
We do & do not want to hear what they heard.
Krankemann laughed....

So, I've orchestrated another story from the year I was born,
1940, even if even the most corpulent ones,
as this one of Krankemann,

cannot be birthed or thinned into knowledge, or even hate.
The obscenely obese sadist
rides my roller

over the square at Auschwitz as though born for it.
He enjoys the work. It whets
his appetite.

History

Evening. I sat at the dining room table, working with tongs, sorting a shoebox of German stamps that had reached me a few months before from Switzerland after an internet auction.

I found dozens of glassines thickly packed with issues ranging from the 1850s to my own century's end. Below the glassines, too, were a few inches of loose stamps, used & mint. Thousands of *Briefmarken* in my horde. As I sorted, I was excited, alive. I realized that my American dollars had gone a long way.

As a boy I spent much time with my stamps. But now, sorting, a different childhood memory kept crowding in until I wondered why: hour after hour, I was at my microscope, tilting its mirror to catch the indoor or outdoor light, eyedroppering pondwater onto slides, staring, surprised by the dimensions I could keep focusing into view. Just when I thought I'd located every organism in a particular drop, another amoeba or paramecium appeared, or a grotesque & fearsome hydra that startled me....

Now, time passed quickly. I was tonging various stamps into various groups. I mounted some in my albums, placed others in stockbooks, others in new glassines that I arranged in numerical Michel catalogue order in my files. There were the shield varieties of the early confederation, & many Germanias of the early empire, & a great many of the inflation issues of the 1920s, but I am most interested in the issues of the Third Reich.

I found several of the death's mask Reinhardt Heydrich, the "Blond Beast" whose assassination led to the annihilation of a village in Czechoslovakia, Lidice, & most of its inhabitants. But of all the propaganda stamps from this period, the greatest quantity were those of the variously-sized & -colored Hitler heads....

As I grew tired & my eyes began to cross, I hoped at least to organize all the stamps in this particular series, but it seemed that no matter how long I sorted through the glassines & then the loose stamps at the bottom of the shoebox—all this history emanating from the center of Europe—there was always another right-facing profile of the Fuhrer. Each time he appeared, he seemed smug, enriddled, immortal, not at all surprised to have reached light again, to have made his way even to America. Each time he appeared, I realized I'd never be able to isolate & bring into focus all the animals in this pond.

Illumination Graft

"a section of the hospital was used
for research into
the effects of castration followed

by cross-gender grafting
of the reproductive glands." ...
"In the operating theatre,

illumination was provided by
several moveable lamps
and a large, fixed, central light."

If

If the Nazis had been left to their devices, if they had kept on,
as Laurence Rees phrases it, with "the process
of turning mass murder into an ordered profession"—

for think of Commandant Stangl arriving at Treblinka in 1942,
realizing that his predecessor's primary problem in making
the camp run smoothly was the capacity of the gas chambers

(bodies were littered all over, trains waited to be unloaded,
the stench was unbearable, the corruption & licentiousness
& frequent ineptitude among Kapos & even SS intolerable),

& think of Stangl building a much larger gassing facility with
"a central corridor off which ran eight separate small gas chambers,"
each of which "could be accessed from outside, which meant that

"clearing them of corpses would be much easier than before,"
total capacity becoming over 3,000 Jews, more than
six times greater than previously possible—

if the SS had gone on to evolve, had had the time
to perfect its process, again, to quote Rees, "of turning
mass murder into an *ordered* profession" (italics mine),

German universities might have offered a major in this,
German students might have received degrees in this
with doctoral dissertations on various human fertilizers, on

efficacious recovery of jewels from particular orifices,
on pacifying vermin children during their procession into the gas,
on creating a hygienic work environment ... as trains

kept arriving from further & further. Pre-Stangl chaos
was not to be endured. Professionals were needed,
an ordered workplace of which the Reich might be proud.

The Soldier

That year when the American taught at a university in the still divided Germany, he would sometimes take long bike rides into the countryside. Sometimes, he would find a path into pine & oak woods & follow it, an adventurer. Twice, at the ends of these paths, he came upon memorials for the country's soldiers fallen in WWII.

The first was a cenotaph stained with birdlime & the tannic residues of leaves. Even its black-letter inscriptions were smeared to the point of unintelligibility. This melancholy geometric seemed to be a mutant tree, unsuccessful in nature, that would sow no seeds & would soon fall & rot. Biking away, he felt an historical gloom lift from him, & noticed that pillars of sunlight created an effect as of temples in the woods behind him.

But it was the second memorial that remained in his mind as for months he worked on his lectures. A great granite bier had blocked his path. On the bier, on his back & staring up into a ring of oaks, was a 12-foot bronze *Wehrmacht* soldier, his eyes still open. From helmet to rifle-across-chest to boot-heels, he was burnished, & shone. It was as though the trees dared not drop leaves on him, the birds dared not insult him. Around the bier had been constructed, too, what seemed to be a marble kneeling-rail. One could kneel, or a child could stand, & reach up to the soldier's shoulder or hip or thigh.

There would never be disintegration here. This soldier would remain a bronze idea, imperishable, determined in his immutability, in his blood-promise, still, to defend the Fatherland.

Sunlight

Within what Anthony Hecht calls "that domain of art" some have said say nothing Rabbi Irving Greenberg says say nothing that cannot/should not be said / that is not "credible in the presence of the burning children" / do they even exist or hear us these injunctions quail us / he does not say credible to *them* but we will let's not bore them not expect too little of them not fear to take chances coo or rave go wild with/for them tell them even their own searing stories— the poet Zelda asks "Are stories my fortress?"—even trust them to forgive us do they even exist Emerson wanted above all wildness from the poet after 'the child is dead' he said to little Louisa May Alcott who came to his door to inquire after his Waldo her little friend died five years old his father's grief yes of rued human "evanescence and lubricity" but his child was dead he could not it might be break out of his iambic wail / but these children were burning from lorries dumped at the Auschwitz pit the boy Eliezer Wiesel could not believe his eyes at pitch night his first day there in the German camp in Poland the Germans their language were burning the Jewish children they'd murdered

& locate young Raul Hilberg Holocaust scholar each morning for three years setting up a bridge table in his parents' NYC apartment writing in pencil chapter after chapter when *when* would he be finished his mother asked him his father *when* would sigh now *The Destruction of the European Jews* revised & expanded the three slipcased freightcar volumes & now several decades later Hilberg's testament *The Politics of Memory* his "The words that are thus written take the place of the past; these words, rather than the events themselves, will be remembered" yes we've not wanted to know this matrix where art/poetry their maws open Hilberg within his work discovering "a primordial act that had not been imagined before it burst forth" Hilberg within his work listening as he wrote to Mozart & Beethoven creating *The*

Destruction a work of art he said Claude Lanzmann told him that to "portray" the Holocaust we have to make art I hear so-called survivor Paul Steinberg in *Speak You Also* say "Those of us who couldn't bow low enough have long ago gone up in smoke" the poet will finally bow low enough to art as master won't he or die by the vertiginous compromise Walt Whitman says "Dazzling and tremendous how quick the sun-rise would kill me, / If I could not now and always send sun-rise out of me" so picture Hilberg up early and/or writing late at his parents' bridge table a graduate student hearing Schubert's Quartet in C "a Germanic work" he says & hearing Beethoven's *Appassionata* "that supreme achievement of piano music" as he raged/prayed for/intensified toward "overall symmetry" balanced harmonies e.g. he says "It was the *andante* of my composition, with a theme and multiple variations that mirrored the special conditions under which deportations were carried out in each country" we hear a fallacy of means here of form this "mirrored" just theory / voltage in writing is not electrified barbed wire nor my statics here but Hilberg composing/conducting his art-text no less than no more than a child at Terezin coloring a butterfly the Jews the facts of the Jews the suffocating vomitous shit-running data of deathtrains the Jews but the point is Hilberg's … radical … acceptance … that art was his meaning his theme did he always know this / when have *you* learned it / as the Germans conducted the Jews these children to the gas within Hilberg's uncovered schedules the SS officers that depravity Mengele with his chic faddish conductor's baton his symphony the lovely child Rachel held her stuffed companion as tightly as she could but in the gas her bear clawed free of her / she held her bear as tightly as she could / but in the gas her bear clawed free of her despite

Nach Auschwitz, ein Gedicht zu schreiben ist barbarisch Adorno is of course correct the manipulations / resolutions / pettinesses/

pretensions/artificialities / failures / loves or so-called successes
of art remain obscene given the perpetrators acting out the horror
of their natures their educations burning the children some alive
burning pyres of families the *Mussulmen* digging ditches out from the
strata necessitated sluices to draw off the human fat make some kind
of music of these brain lobes these furrows? some kind of paintings?
sculptures? poems? Adorno is correct who later tempered his tongue
begrudged we needed to have our say I say Adorno was right to begin
with & wrong & correct when he tempered his speech & wrong for
here's Czeslaw Milosz that exile who said time came when he knew
earth could not be his home nor any hereafter but here he is in *The
Witness of Poetry* & he is correct & he is wrong he says "Whoever
invokes genocide, starvation, or the physical suffering of our fellow
men in order to attack poems or paintings practices demogoguery"
/ & then our next inevitable step toward our only hope our despair
toward the supremacy of art as when Lawrence Langer recognizes
the "void of discord" atrocity knowledge visits on us—(my word,
visits, & the right one, I only *visit* these materials which yes always
shadow me but I am visitor my grandchildren will visit me this
weekend e.g. & we'll have light & air I only *visited* Bergen-Belsen the
one *Konzentrazionslager* on whose ground I have in body stood Anne
I had your diary in me there but we only *visit* in fact Erich Neumann
in his essay "Meaning and Man" says "one million Jewish children
could be slaughtered with no great impact on mankind—not on
psychologists, theologians, believers or unbelievers, from the Pope to
the Communists" he doesn't mention the poets but we too visit but
some poems can stay longer can stay always that duration of art)—
Langer knows we can no longer aspire to "the utopian humanistic
enlightenment we once dreamed of achieving" but, but, but still says
"no oral testimonies so far equal the *art* of writers like Primo Levi,
Aharon Appelfeld, Charlotte Delbo, and Ida Fink to name only a
few" he too on the visceral slope toward art whatever art no matter

what despite its myriad pre-emptions/egotisms its sometimes semi-trances of illusory coherence despite its ... *beauty* ... / Fink's baker Weizkranz old & sick stuffed into a barrel the details endlessly varying as his story is told how he was rolled until dead he rolls unto death variations on a nocturnal theme this art while his camp's commandant after the war sells smoked meat & the kapo that "dog in charge of all the other dogs" becomes white-collar while Weizkranz is a kind of music isn't he our way toward the *the* of this melody's domain of barrel staves on gravel Fink says he "for maybe even years, will keep rising from the dead and dying in the barrel" notice "maybe" as operative word *maybe* if we can see/hear him can we will I or you or will we weary of/recoil from this flour-shrouded memory—in one of Fink's story-plays (a Jewish couple long in hiding) a woman says "There was an oriole who used to sing in our garden" but the man answers "Klara, no memories. Remember our bargain"— but how the baker enfigures himself into art-memory his strength from being shaped by the barrel the "paradoxical imperatives" in Jay Ladin's terms of its staves that musical form nothing no sound getting in to him except the sound of the crushed gravel the snails crushed underfoot at Glasnevin where Gerard Manley Hopkins is buried father the baker brings you his bread the kingfisher blood from his ear the music of this foot-crushed stave-crushed gravel don't touch me you brutal foot you bastard the form-enfolded Weizkranz the baker demands of me from his elsewhere tell me my story he regurgitates the nothing within him our art this barrel becomes him & churches are shells discarded by God in Ladin's poem "Snails" as our maker "with horns and a single foot / ... crawls over the world" / Weizkranz is it true your knuckles broke your kneecaps broke your clavicles broke like snailshells underfoot & how the perpetrators hide in my own habitual syntax *they* your knuckles broke kneecaps clavicles the merciless ones the barrel of history crushes music into that gravel

   & how in *The Primal Mind* Jamake Highwater describes his

efforts to discover "communicative accesses" toward breaking barriers between the dominant culture & the Other (what else were Lakota to the dominant culture but vermin?) could only be by way of "the metaphoric form of expression called 'art' in the West" he says "if someone does not experience an aesthetic relationship to what is before him or her, all the information and education will not permit that person to cross the distance that exists between different peoples" but what "aesthetic relationship" with smallpox blankets & bayoneted genitals but Highwater's faith & what else is it that we might aspire to except to / break down, break down again my songs where the lorry of murdered children draws up at the firepit the boy Elie needs us 50-60 years later in *A Jew Today* he'll write "If you have not grasped it until now, it is time you did: Auschwitz signifies death— total, absolute death—of man and of mankind, of reason and of the heart, of language and of the senses. Auschwitz is the death of time, the end of creation; its mystery is doomed to stay whole, inviolate" but despite art he keeps writing he resists writing he mentions Rabbi Mendel of Kotzk who was silent even when speaking what is all this but a selfish defense of poetry which cannot / can it be spoken *credibly* in the presence of the burning children do they even exist my failure & you with me too in this "mystery" Wiesel says & Herman Melville's biblical *II Thessalonians*, 7 phrase "mystery of iniquity" rises to him from beneath John Claggart's black breastbone Jay Ladin's utterly forlorn & surrendering phrase "an evil that beggars cognition" & *is* evil ineradicable our natural essence each cell stained the smoker's lungs that will never regain the rose color of fleshly innocence even after the smoker stops smoking for sixty years the crematoria or can Highwater's "aesthetic relationship" as Hilberg composes *Destruction* be of some even slight assuagement of the darker angels of our nature Satan of the darkest order I don't/can't know but do know & the answer is *no* but know that the most encouraged I am in this history is when I read that many brainwashed *Einsatzgruppen* went mad/committed suicide could not after all continue / something of what we hopefully even prayerfully call the *human* welling up in them after the first murder & after the 100th & 500th it is not that there is no other but that the Other *is* another an other & the German soldier sometimes despite Hitler *und Vaterland und* his drunken comrades broke down from the radiant stain of his conscience may our natures now modulate ever into benign forms is there time on earth will our brains allow us break down again my crazed songs & for now give me joy you murderers of my own blood kill yourselves you're human after all my only lifeline your suicides splatter your acidic hearts here on my pages even while ours is Susan Gubar's poetry after Auschwitz please do I hope in the end to locate myself there "this task of abjuring the redemptive paradigm" / I hope as I abjure hope because of my hope nevertheless & may you be strong songs, my songs, worthy company in this mystery this "opacity" as Susan Sontag says & may you be at least sometimes unselfconscious but true to me & may you be at least sometimes poetry the black liquid that seeps from the muse's eye-sockets if I'd been born not in Brooklyn in 1940 but Berlin in 1920 I'd have aspired to the SS from that culture my German-born parents wished the Jews the worst I was a blond youth tall an athlete I'd have sworn allegiance to/murdered for/cut off my fingers for that incarnation of Reich savior he of the "luminous blue eyes" as Goebbels wrote in his diary on first meeting him how could/can I resist that blood-anthem hypnagogic rapture for whom I'd raze villages slaughter innocence but then I hope get drunk then I hope press the curved trigger-stave the barrel of my rifle against my shell my razed temple & fire before he takes me here eat this new grotesque beautiful formful poem this visitor this /

Shoah Goat

My dream, the goat rears up on its back legs.
Come here in human moonlight, I cannot

see it straight on. Looking to the side of it,
& to the side of the side of it, I can almost see it,

but only so far as my fear allows—its leather
horns smoldering, its chin slavered with viscera,
its lurid cock shining with Jew-spittle & blood,
its cleft eyes blue & crossing now to remember.

I did not nor you we are not guilty must insist despite translucent
possibilities of fallibility & brainwashed complicity I did not was not
there nor you we did not murder the lorries of children dumped into
the burning pit do not never we must not Anthony Hecht must not
have thought this through misread who praised *The Swastika Poems* for
reaching "that domain of art in which criminal and victim, caught in
the light of a steady vision, are virtually the same" I'd beg the dead's
forgiveness but did not write this no there is no such "domain of
art" did I write this / this is not May Sarton's journal entry "I cannot
separate Germans from Nazis" her sense however right or wrong
or however to be modulated Goldhagen's argument of national
complicity but this says starkly Cain *is* Abel no I did not lyric this
but yes I have sometimes accused undercut recoiled from their God
on whose assumed keep they suffered who was not there with them
or witnessed & did not lift an eyelid to keep them Rachel held her
bear as tightly as she could / but in the gas her bear clawed free
of her / break down break down again my songs / Whitman says
despite everything the half-holy cosmic one unexiled despite holding
the young dead & dying in his arms the piles of amputated limbs
at Fredericksburg notwithstanding his imagination & soul sickness
& being there says "I believe the soggy clods shall become lovers
and lamps" his own domain but goodbye Walt after the Shoah's
deathcamps we depart for our residence now the beloved child has
not in this duration died of Scarlatina but is murdered we reside exiled

in Ladin's "revulsion against the very texture of the aesthetic"—for decades I didn't think so but in the end it's about me isn't it?—but let's stop stuffing this bear stop gassing it for who does not want even Celan wanted with his imploded incandescences his backwhorling from *dass was geschah* that which happened wanted & Levi who says in an interview he'd revise Adorno to "after Auschwitz it is barbaric to write poetry except about Auschwitz" / & Wiesel & Hilberg & Ozick in *The Shawl* & Jean-Francois Steiner in *Treblinka* & Samuel Bak in his candle-crematoria paintings & Joyce Carol Oates in her novel *The Gravedigger's Daughter* & Markus Zusak in *The Book Thief* all wanted/ want don't they or I'm deluded don't they at once *both* in Gubar's terms want "heartfelt and personal reactions to the disaster" *&* texts the same texts that cannot be fully sounded cannot be exhausted *will* in Ladin's terms "invite & repay critical attention to the work they do" even as we know our best work our art only visits for now while weak poems puddle & imply they know / but art is now cadaverous with man's ultimate architectures the deathcamps after the Shoah we humbly/egotistically reside with this it could be when we become most human an unstylized knowledge this extremity of exile from the fields & trees of the oriole in our only possible /

Sunlight

This is what we've learned: victim
Miklòs Radnòti's poems
(the ones exhumed from a mass grave
after the war before their notebook could rot)

would have been better off if
left in the pit whose contents mis-
understood them but kept teaching them
that language we living can't speak.

Loyalty

He dreamed a city in ruins. Dogs fought over a corpse. He was that corpse, staring upward, slavering mongrels tearing at his senseless legs, & he was not, but saw everything from where he stood, his arms folded across his chest as though he would have nothing to do with this.

How had it happened that this metropolis had been reduced to rubble? Where were all its citizens? Its one inhabitant, the dead one now seeming to represent what had once been its teeming population, had no answers for him.

His chest began to ache. Even if in so doing he would merely be reprising an infinite number of such romantic memorial gestures, he felt he needed to kick the dogs away from that corpse. He unfolded his arms in case he would need them to protect his throat. Later, hopefully, there would be time for him to bury or burn what was left of the oblivious one.

Autumn Rain, 1946

Then Goering crunched down hard on a filling
under which a cyanide capsule burst.
Maybe a minute of agony, & then death,
at Nuremberg, on his own terms.
Those who would hang came to envy him.

Hermann had grown so fat that wolverines followed
in his shadow to gorge on him in case
he fell. No, they didn't. But he did grow obese,
& his huge hunting lodge filled with Third Reich swag.
O those unforgettable social evenings of elegance & grog.

You've heard the saying that it's hard to predict history.
I'm writing it now, as you are while hearing this.
Who knows who is going to say what about us
as time comes to pass? Of course, we'd both rather be
on the side of the seers, so please plan on revising me.

By now everyone knows that cyanide
permeates the corpse that smells of almond.
I heard that Goering died in his pajamas, with his boots on
that so often strutted beside the Fuhrer's
as rapt throngs witnessed their strides toward suicide.

Those were of course the finest Italian leather boots
Germany could afford. Their raised heels
shaped calves, thighs, buttocks into firm
Aryan shapes that a shapeless nation
might model. But our hero became so flaccid

II

A Poetics of Hiroshima

Judgment

In 1855 Walt Whitman rhapsodized that the great poet
"*is* judgment. He judges not as the judge judges,
but as the sun falling around a helpless thing."

Today, the sun is falling. Today Custer attacks
an Indian village on the Washita to slaughter
whole families. The sun falls on him as around

a helpless thing, does it. Today's is an aftersun,
long after. "From a sufficient perspective,"
said Ralph Waldo Emerson, "everything pleases,"

so today we're pleased, are we, as Custer & his troops
butcher infants & their elders, our perspective
being sufficient, & the aftermoon, too,

falls around the 7th Cavalry as around a helpless thing.
We are far away, we are so far away that we cannot
smell burning hair clotted with blood. Moon

& sun fall on murderers as around helpless things
as all becomes known, all comes to eventual judgment,
does it, as aftersoul envelops all helpless things.

Iwo Dahlia

My high school coach of the mid-Fifties—
he brought us a dahlia, a single purple bloom
my wife and I have floating in a glass bowl on our kitchen table.
Add a couple ice cubes a couple times a day, he said,
and it should keep, as it has, except for corolla petals
now curling blackly downward.

A few years back he gave us a babyfood jar of sand from Iwo Jima.
With six hundred other veterans, he'd returned a half-century after
hitting the beach there, burying his face in this volcanic grit.
At Marine reunions, he can't find anyone from his old outfit.
Dahlia, that widower grandfather now trusts his memories to you.
May you distill color from even blackpurples, and remember.

Autumn means digging up their tubers, wrapping them in burlap,
carrying them to his rural cellar where the mysterious
dormant life in them will overwinter. They need cold,
but he'll check them several times to make sure the ice
or insects or mice haven't found them out.
There's no sump pump, and usually his hard-packed dirt floor—

I've been down there—retains an inch or two of rain,
but he's constructed a path of raised flagstones,
can make his way, he tells me, even without a flashlight,
through the dark to the cabinet where his dahlias sleep.
The promise of them again is always in his mind,
and has been, and will be, one way or another....

D-Night at Iwo Jima was cold, the wounded shuddering,
medics brushing black sand from stumps and bandages.
Six hundred Marines were dead already—the Japanese

had sited their artillery onto the beaches months before,
were hidden behind revetments in mountain caves
and deep tunnels, were seldom seen that day.

Safe civilian litter-bearer, I'll haul Coach's dahlia
to our compost back of the garden, and spade it in, but not yet.
It will lose its colors, its seared purples going to sepia and black
as it edges in on itself, collapses, and begins to smell,
but not yet. For now, whole, it concentrates October light,
seems to sense the silver maple leaffall outside our window....

Inland that first day, a medic plunged into a shellhole,
then looked around. Next to him, the detached arm
of a dead Marine, its wristwatch keeping time, gold band
shining in Iwo sun, 4,000 miles from Pearl Harbor. Dahlia,
transform to gold, keep memorial time. I'm standing again
above the *Arizona*: 1,000 dead, average age nineteen....

Rear Admiral Toshinosuke Ichimaru, commander
of this island named for its springs of sulfur,
to venerate His Majesty the Emperor wrote poetry.
He prayed Hirohito live as long as sacred Mount Fuji.
Grateful to be placed where he could die
against the American assault, he wrote:

> *In the twilight the waters of Lake Hamana cool,*
> *Sending breezes to fill my garden,*
> *Fragrant with sweet oleanders in full bloom.*
> *Let me fall like the flower petals scatter.*
> *May enemy bombs aim at me, and enemy shells*
> *Mark me as their target....*

Tonight, those petals scattered, rain seeps
into my teacher's cellar,
but he is there again, walking on flagstones.
He unwraps burlap and fingers the dirt-crusted tubers.
May he be able, long as he lives, to bear these dahlias
whose names are myriad, whose target is his heart,

but who can?—there is too much in him, all night
white and amber and green-suffused flares
color Suribachi, lives leak through gauze into black sand,
flamethrowers wait on the color-coded beaches in dreamfumes
of burning Japanese meat and the suffocation to be visited
on these unbelievers with revengeful biblical fury....

In the jungle battles at Bougainville and Guam,
men died out of sight, sank into foliage and swamp quietly.
On Iwo Jima, men died in full view, torn apart,
their bones and viscera spraying and splattering,
shrapnel slashing into them as their last thoughts
flew toward the silence of the past, and home.

On Wednesday, the last day of February, 1945,
their tenth day ashore, the Marines held less than half the island.
Hand-to-hand combat in the central hills—
no survivor will describe this terror.
Where is the old man when he is in his cellar
and shuts his eyes and touches the cemetery of dahlia?

In spring, when all chance of frost is past,
Coach plants them in staggered rows, six inches deep,
one tuber per cedar stake, stakes two feet apart,
rows six feet apart so he'll have room to groom and tend.
You lay each tuber down, he says,

with its eye-end toward the stake, pointing up....

The single dahlia head in its bowl sometimes
seems to weigh more than its table can support,
evening light fused with sepals and petaltips,
notes of taps lost in its empurpled and disfigured inwardness,
Time's harvest now, waking and sleep equal,
as though its presence were a cave being sealed from us.

The night sky lit with dead stars, a jugular vein pierced,
but a medic kneels to the panic, slits the bullet hole,
lays the vein bare and clamps it, stuffs the hole with gauze,
holds it tight. Lips pressed closed, he prays
that this day's battle be god's will. Enfold this tableau,
dahlia, succor the striken soldier and his savior....

Wrapped in tissue in a small oblong box under shirts
in a drawer in a chest in a bedroom in a house
off a road in a town in a county in a state
of our country, under a ribbon and stars, George Washington
faces left in profile on a Purple Heart. He's thinking
of his wife and Mount Vernon. He seldom sees the light....

I dreamed countless *sennimbari*,
cotton bands of a thousand stitches
worn around their waists by Japanese soldiers,
each stitch a prayer for their return.
I coughed a belt, a clot of *sennimbari*,
woke from a vomit of blood and magma....

Can the dead remember, Iwo dahlia?
Where were you, what garden preserved you
when their ravines received the flaming oil?

From even this distance, from the safety of our grief,
you still smolder, your tuberous nature wrapped in burlap,
your eyes inured to that incendiary sun,

and sweet water, and the essence of the living who were there.
You depose the sacramental rose, do you, and the dooryard lilac
smug with pastoral remembrance, and the Japanese oleander
whose commander rhapsodized his suicidal honor.
Dahlia, you've lost your heavy heads to mortars,
your petals shrapnel the neck of our hourglass....

Near the end, the fight in the northeast, a Marine lay over
a sulfur fissure, the hot mephitic stench
seeming to help stanch his fatal wound;
here, dahlia, bleed in your bowl,
enemies slash the ears from your helmeted head,
pull your teeth with pliers for souvenirs....

Two months after D-Day a journalist visited Iwo, noticed
big blue flies clinging to broken limbs, "so numerous
and so close they almost touch. They don't hover or buzz.
They just cling. Brushing a limb barely starts them.
They just cling, surfeited." E.B. Hadfield deployed that word,
surfeited, as though the flies were fat and drowsy with gore,

the blue flies and dead limbs a grotesque parody, he said,
Iwo Japanese flower arrangement. Here, then,
the ceremony of dahlia: viscous lacquer pacific pour
of surfeited flies into a cup of porcelain hemlock
as Coach, asleep, or kneeling in his floating cellar,
breathes deep, and resists, but remembers....

When the U.S. returned the island to Japan—1968—
Coach's dahlias surrendered in ironic gloom,
downcellar, in burlap, in his cabinet,
but fought above ground in full gear, but didn't.
He was with them when he was not with them,
living what had once been theirs, life in light.

Back on Iwo, lagged and blitzed, he rode a shuttle
up from crosses to the summit of Suribachi's cone
where bushes and grass camouflaged pillbox rubble.
He'd carried with him a dozen miniature Old Glories
and now pushed them into the mountain, stood at attention,
then packed them for disabled vets at home....

In the battle between oleander and dahlia
in this way in the perfection of Time
Coach has asked me to darken his ashes
with Iwo Jima's volcanic sand
and scatter the mixture, half over his wife's grave—
she who wept with his fear—half in the sea....

Today, Coach walks in elegy above his cellar.
In the synaptic concussions of his daydream, we hear ...
but no one can listen there except dead friends from photos
of fifty years before. Rocket trucks liquid as plasma,
it may be, weeping solid as bullets, time's divisions un-
raveling to Time's seamless and deathless will;

meanwhile, below ground, in case, cold keeps his ammo.
Which of us would question him, or them,
given the simple faith of dahlia in full beauty and attack?
Spring spirals, never-arriving until, by way of a soldier's valor,
it will. His seasons return, commodious black,
perpetual witness with this flower.

The Plugs

On August 6, 1945, shortly after the *Enola Gay* rose from its runway on Tinian Island in the Pacific, Morris Jepson descended into the bomb bay to commence arming our weapon nick-named "Little Boy."

This is what I read this morning in a newspaper. Jepson changed the bomb's "plugs," then the *Enola Gay* rose to 30,000 feet & at 8:15 a.m. its pilot, Col. Paul W. Tibbetts, gave the order, & that was that, 90,000 dead soon after, another 145,000 within months, etcetera.

I'm thinking about this 60 years later. If you're like me, you're too numb from all our wars to care, or care very much, but those plugs, metal or hard rubber, whatever shape they were & however many, whether threaded into apertures or hammered into place or welded, whatever size they were, do interest us—their occluded density, the gagged occluded sound of them, their color, how they might have felt in Jepson's hands, their metallic or rubbery odor in his mind as he concentrated on his task, as the American weapon assumed its consequential form. Before now, no poem or prose piece has received them, has welcomed these plugs in their material innocence, their muteness, in their full utilitarian nature, home. They served us, parts of the whole, & having served us, when "Little Boy" detonated 1,890 feet above the city, our plugs disappeared into the micro-afterdust of uranium, into almost nothingness.

Almost. Except that we breathe these microcosmic particles, our lungs filter & distribute these plugs minute by minute, breath by breath.

The *Enola Gay* sailed through the atomic flash & got back to its base. The plane still exists, entire, itself another dimension of plug, the names of its 12-man crew stencilled on its fuselage. I haven't yet seen it, but maybe will, on exhibition in the Smithsonian or wherever it will be. But whether or not I ever see it, or you ever see it, doesn't much matter. What matters is that word with which Jepson was working & which we cannot/will not forget or replace.

The next time you push a plug into a socket. The next time you fish for bass or pickeral with a plug. The next time you hear a plug for a politician. Hold the word in hand &/or mind. Hiroshima. *Guh*, at the back of the throat. *Guh*. August 6, 1945. Morris Jepson changes "Little Boy's" plugs.

The Streetcar: August 6, 1945

For several hours just after the atomic bombing of Hiroshima,
        a professional photographer,

Yoshito Matsushige, wandered the city, taking five pictures,
        not taking many others,

as when he walked up to & looked inside a streetcar jammed
        with dead passengers.

"They were all in normal positions," Yoshito said, "holding
        onto straps, sitting

"or standing still, just as they were before the bomb went off.
        Except that all

"leaned in the same direction—away from the blast. And all
        were burned black,

"a reddish black, and they were stiff." Yoshito put one foot
        up on the streetcar,

raised & focused his camera, fingered the shutter, but
        did not take this picture....

This streetcar with its stiff reddish-black & leaning passengers
        now travels our city,

stops & starts at crossings for our relentless traffic. Behind
        the dutiful driver,

no one is going shopping or visiting old parents or working figures
  on an abacus

or remembering a poem by an ancient master. We must not question
  or detain them, must not

stop this streetcar with our ideas in order to accept or understand,
  or to take their picture.

if HST had not given the order.
As a participant in necessary atrocity, I agreed.
I still agree. But it doesn't matter if I agree—
what matters is whether poetry itself agrees. Incidentally,
Ashida was in training to become
a divine wind, a kamikaze.

1945. I was almost five. Col. Tibbets named
our *Enola Gay* for his mother.
The 6th of August. Our bomb, "Little Boy," mushroomed
with the force of 15 kilotons of TNT.
"A harnessing of the basic power of the universe," said HST,
as though the universe were our plowhorse.
In the woman's home, her daughter was beheaded.
I don't know if Ashida learned exactly how,
though we & the art of atrocity would like to know.
In any case, what could this mother do?
She lifted her daughter's head. She laid it
in the aforementioned jewel-center.
She was not thinking of the basic power of the universe.
Did she place oleander blossoms on her baby's face?
Did she enfold her daughter's head in silk, which rhymes with *bucket*,
& *sick*, & *volcanic*, & *wreak havoc*? …

(Buckets appear often, as a matter of fact,
in the literature of exile, for example
in Irina Ratushinskaya's prison memoir *Gray is the Color
of Hope*—coal buckets & slop buckets,
ersatz food placed in what were toilet buckets.
"Time to get up, woman. Empty your slop bucket."
Irina drags her bucket daily to the cess pit.
She doesn't know if she can ever become a mother.)

Ashida attained the highest black belt, went on
to coach the American Olympic judo team.
He did. I spoke with his daughter
at an event where I received a poetry prize,
a check for a thousand George Washingtons
& an etched glass compote
for a book on the Shoah. I said I once heard her father
lecture on Zen—the moon in the river,
River flowing by that is the world with its agonies
while Moon remains in one place,
steadfast despite atrocity.
I remember that she seemed at ease,
she who had known her father
as I could never.

While teaching at the University of Hawaii,
I visited Pearl Harbor three times, launched out to the memorial
above the *Arizona*. Below us, the tomb
rusted away—a thousand sailors,
average age nineteen—for nature, too, is atrocity,
atoms transformed within it, even memory.
We tourists, some Japanese, watched minnows
nibble at our leis.
No, we did not. This was my dream:
I knelt at a rail under a Japanese officer with a sword,
but now there are too many stories for poetic safety,
for stanzaic integrity—woman & daughter,
Ashida at his lecture, my high school coach carrying heads
of dahlias grown from bulbs
he'd kept in burlap to overwinter in his cellar,
even persona Heyen at Pearl Harbor

above the rusting & decalcifying battleship that still breathed
bubbles of oil that still
iridesced the Pacific swells as jewel-centers iridesce
our most anthologized villlanelles....

A bombing survivor said, "It's like when you burn
a fish on the grill."

I end my sixth line above with the word "home."
My first draft called it the woman's "house," but *home*
evokes satisfaction, *mmm*, a baby's
contentment at the breast, the atrocity
of irony, & *home* hears itself in *arm,* & *bomb,* & *blossom,*
& looks forward to *shame* & *tomb.*
I cannot not tell a lie.
Apparently, I am not so disgusted with atrocity
as I'd claimed to be—my atoms
do not cohere against detonation, but now time has come—listen
to the *mmm* in *time* & *come*—for closure,
as, out of the azure,

into the syntax of Hiroshima, "Little Boy" plunges—
I've centered this poem both to mushroom
& crumble its edges—
& "Fat Man," 21 kilotons of TNT,
will devastate Nagasaki. What is your history? Please don't leave
without telling me. Believe me,
I'm grateful for your enabling complicity.
I know by now you've heard my elegiac ē.
I hope your exiled mind has bucketed its breath.
I seek to compose intellectual melody.
I fuse my fear with the idea of the holy.

This is St. John's *cloud of unknowing* in me.
This is the Tao of affliction in me.
Don't try telling me my poetry is not both
beguiling & ugly.

"There was no escape except to the river," a survivor said.
but the river thronged with bodies.
Black rain started falling, covering everything the survivors said.

I have no faith except in the half-life of poetry.
I seek radiation's rhythmic sublime.
I have no faith except in atrocity.
I seek the nebulous ends of time.
This is the aria those cities have made of me.
I hope my centered lines retain their integrity.
I have no faith except in beauty.

Beauty

She told me that during the Second World War
she'd found herself on a Pacific island.
One hot morning, walking forest patched out
by bombs & Seabee dozers, she came upon
the corpse of an enemy soldier. Apparently,

some days before, after a nearby concussion,
he'd crawled from his hole, & died there.
Now, she did taste a fruit-sweet putrescence
in summer air … but what she needed to tell me,
what needed her to tell this story

was that the maggots swilling in the soldier's face
were golden, a beautiful browngold glistening.
When she saw them, her heart unclenched.
She knew, despite everything she'd witnessed,
she could, possibly, be happy again.

Coda to Iwo Dahlia

Here comes Coach again with his dahlias.
It must be autumn, I've been in a dream.
The *Iwo Jima* has had to sail back out
into the Gulf now that "Rita" is bearing down.

Storms of human history, & this year's hurricanes,
& Coach's fire-red & red-purple blooms.
It must be autumn, I've been in a dream.
The old Marine is visiting this home again....

Here & gone, & now these heavy heads
float in clear glass bowls on our tables.
The *Iwo Jima* is riding out the storm,
then will return to flooded New Orleans.

It must be autumn, I've been in a dream.
I hope Coach has made it home again
to where his dahlias will overwinter
in burlap in bushel baskets in his cellar ...

where he'll visit them to speak a comrade's words
even while snow cascades. Every year, again,
he'll harvest faces & find me here.
It must be autumn, I've been in a dream.

teased them into chambers she believed their Palestine—
the children, she was sure, were & would be vermin.
At war's end, her great regret was the program's cessation.

Mandel is almond in German, the smell of this woman
lingering in the history of atrocity like the smell of almond
emanating from corpses from injections of cyanide.

4.
& consider lethally seductive Lieutenant Podust
prowling her web during the early 1980s as the Soviet Union,
in its virulent death throes, rewarded such as she

to perfect skills to turn those who said *No* into animals.
Look into Irina Ratushinskaya's prison memoir *Gray
Is the Color of Hope*, hundreds of pages of suffering by way

of twisted Podust & her superiors who tried to obliterate
Irina's poetry (sometimes scratched with a burnt match on bars
of ersatz soap, memorized, washed off, smuggled out to survive).

Rose

I had a friend who planned to become
a dead poet.

It wasn't easy, but he worked at it
until it

became him & he it, lungs & heart
& Rilkean

attar of swoon in his oxygen tubes.
I loved him,

it wasn't easy, but I worked at it
until it

did seem, didn't it, that dying spring,
a kind of song

between us, as if I might, after all, not
survive him?

Rainer Maria writes long letters
from his castles,

I hope my friend can still receive them,
though I cannot,

though an occasional streaked blossom still
seems to fall.

Fledgling

I then listened to a catbird about everything
under the shade. The catbird mewed
sound sequences close to singing,
but not song, unless song remains, at best,
arhythmic melody; unless melody remains,
at best, only rents & fragments, only
the gasped ingestion of *Zyklon B.*

From here, this evening, I sense her nesting
in my forehead. Any surviving baby
will soon be fledgling twirling among
honeysuckle leaves & berries,
as she does, when she is not singing,
or not lisping sounds that once were song.
We might hear such remembering

as is possible from black & gray smoke filtering
into trees that still host them every spring,
& will, except they do not seem nearly
as confident as sometimes my deluded meanings
used to be, it may be. Whoever you are,
I write you to revise me in the aftertime
for hearing what was never the catbird's song.

Blueberries Album

1.

A bucket of previously unrecorded black & white preliberation Auschwitz photos has been uncovered. I've tasted some of them online. They are of the SS & their *Helferinnen*, the female auxilliary. It seems that all these personages are having a good time, relaxing from their duties.

2.

A July 22, 1944 snapshot shows a group of eleven *Helferinnen* sitting on a railing on an outdoor deck. They are with officer Karl Höcker. They have just now finished eating their bowls of blueberries.

3.

During my boyhood, wild blueberries grew in abundance along the sand-edged tar roads in Nesconset in the center of Long Island. Once in a while, I'd stop my bike for a handful on a summer day. My mind wants to go back to those days now.

4.

Once, hiding from a friend, I knelt in a thicket of blueberries & was stung by a bumblebee. I'd often been stung by yellowjackets, & once by a hornet, but this bumblebee sting—well, while I'm thinking of it now, my left temple buzzes a little where the bee got me about 55 years ago. No kidding: nerves between cheekbone & ear remember that yellow & black & reddish-pink—the flowers of the blueberry are reddish-pink—jolt.

5.

This photo from Raul Hilberg's *The Destruction of the European Jews*: "The corpses were pink in color, with green spots." These were the gassing victims at Auschwitz.

16.

There must have been caches of Hungarian blueberries in the freight cars. Some children must have been pacified with them. There must have been blueberry vomit & blueberry diarrhea.

17.

It's hard to tell from the photo what time of day it is—maybe mid- or late-afternoon. Maybe, in an hour or two, these personages will all have coffee & an assortment of cakes & ices. & what is in store for them this very evening? There is an air of flirtation in this & other photos.

18.

My mother was born in Bremerhaven on the day WWI started, August 1, 1914. As I write, she is 93, resident in a nursing home just a few miles away from me here in western New York State. Today I asked her if the blueberries in Germany were the same kind as those that grew on the Island, for there are many species. Yes, she said, exactly the same, no question about it. She said that she & her several sisters & her brother would pick them, that her mother would boil them into syrup for pancakes, & also mix them into the batter. She said that her father loved these pancakes, that she herself could still smell them as they sizzled into firmness in her mother's black iron skillets.

19.

The skin of the ripest Nesconset blueberries was not shiny, but smoky, hazy.

20.

How fierce & tough my mother is. She does not want ever to die. She is now angrily recovering from surgery after a second broken hip. She is a force of nature. As long as she is alive, all those Jews are dead, & will stay dead.

21.

My mother said that they were called *Bickberen*. She spelled the word out: B-I-C-K-B-E-R-E-N. But I can't find such a word in my English-German dictionary. Blueberries are identified as *Blaubeere* or *Heidelbeere*. *Blau* is blue, of course; the *Heidel* might go to heather/moor/heath.

22.

The blueberries disappeared from Nesconset roadsides during about the time I went to high school & college. Lawns were planted, & the mauves of lilacs—Walt Whitman's memory bloom— & the yellows of forsythia bushes, & the pinks of ornamental trees as the Suffolk County building boom heightened.

23.

My herbalist says that the leaves & berries of this low shrub are to be mixed a teaspoonful to a cup of boiling water, one or two cups to be imbibed each day, that this is "of great value in diarrhea."

24.

The leaves & flowers of this plant may be useful as an astringent. My dictionary says that an astringent is "a substance that constricts the tissues or canals of the body, thereby diminishing discharges, as of mucus or blood." But there was not enough astringent in the cattle cars to stanch all the discharges of mucus & blood, urine & watery feces. There was not enough in Europe. There is not now enough astrigent in the cosmos to stanch the discharges from the Shoah transports.

25.

Often, thinking about things, we do not want to think about them.

26.

In the *Kabbalah*, colors commence with blue. Blue is first to emerge from black. Blue opens & releases black. I cannot not think about this, but my mind can neither encircle nor penetrate this poetry.

27.

In our Nesconset cellar, my mother submerged white shirts & blouses & socks in a basin of bluing water.

28.

We can't know everything. Maybe one of these women was in emotional & spiritual turmoil, hated herself & her place here, did not brutalize the condemned, could not sleep, forced herself to smile for this photo.

29.

A friend of mine said that once upon a time in the Adirondacks he was alone, picking blueberries, when he heard a rustle in the bushes. A black bear cub emerged. Guess what fearful thought, at that moment, came blueberrying into his mind.

30.

My encyclopaedia says that these days Auschwitz is a center of communications where five railway lines meet.

31.

There would have been no way to escape from the mother bear's jaws.

32.

Blueberry flowers bear five dark blue or black seeds.

33.

Blueberry bushes thrive in acidic soils. But what does my stomach ache matter? What does my writing matter?

34.

Go backward in time from when the color blue first appears in the bush's white berries. Halve that first blue &, however pale, there is still some slight tinge or essence of blue. Halve this slight blue again, & again, & according to the law of infinite divisibility, there is still some blue that will always be there, that was there from the beginning.

35.

Speaking of human nature: think of the SS man who, while drowning a newborn baby under a faucet sang, "There you go, little Moses, down the stream." ... But, no, this might not have been his innate nature. But think of him. Deal with him.

36.

The wild blueberries were fairly small. *Zyklon B* pellets were a half to a third the size of the berries the SS consumed that day; they were porous, chalky, with a slight bluish tinge. *Zyklon B* deteriorated fairly quickly, like blueberries. Hurry, before it is too late, let us refill the bowls of Höcker & these women, this time with those other pellets. But then, who would we be?

37.

I've known from my beginnings that I'll have completed this album only when it can sustain itself on its own blueberries, only when it does not sicken itself.

38.

Höcker & the women are having a wonderful time, it appears. He is hip to hip with them, as I am, our female auxilliaries, my muses, my blueberries.

The Light

The fact is that there occurred discussions among officials
as to whether it would be best
during gassings

to leave lights on in the chambers or turn them off.
I don't know what,
in the end—

for efficiency or for the sensibilities of the ... facilitators—
was decided,
or if,

in fact, a consistent policy existed. In the end,
the insensate entangled innocent
were dragged out

into the Aryan light of the 1940s into which
I was issued from the womb
of a Jew-hater

into the light of gold teeth at this zenith of human time.
The doors open. Dead light
reveals me.

Trying to Get to You

That's what his dream meant: that it wasn't a matter of how much luggage or where it was or where it was supposed to be taken to from among the living room clutter of furniture & legs through which he'd have to step in his bare feet to lift the various mismatched vessels; it wasn't a matter of the snow outside on the way to his vehicle which might or might not have enough space so that more than one trip might or might not be necessary; it wasn't a matter of whether or not anybody there at the dysfunctional house might help him get all the stuff out from under their feet before somebody fell or a child got lost or maimed amid the clunky mess. It was a matter of how he'd gotten to be where he was in the first place, involved in trying to make some kind of order out of the living room so that all the arguing & cursing that the others were doing might have some space for words to be heard instead of colliding with the suitcases & bags & trunks that were filled to bursting with the past, Germany pushing out seams & sutures, emotional diseases emanating from vinyl & leather, wounds leaking blood from out one particular dove-tailed valise his father had made & his mother had used for her curling irons & cosmetics. Yes, why was he here again when by now he should have been mature & powerful enough to put all this behind him? Instead of being absent from this living room & all this unredeemable vitriolic anti-Semitic past, he was still barefoot here & wanting to clear things out of their way. But at least he now knew what he knew. And he had enough money now to be free of them. Maybe he could find his shoes somewhere in all this luggage & get out of here across the snow to his car which would probably start & he could fill it with gasoline & he could put on his headphones & listen to Elvis's Sun Sessions songs & he could drive at last the hell out of here & away from these people to his new home far west of old Brooklyn.

Pitch

In June 1941 at Bialystok,
Poland, 700 Jews were locked
into their synagogue which was then
set on fire. A German police battalion
(*Ordnungspolizei*) ringed this scene,
rifles ready in case someone
might burst out
through a window, or a wall
collapse to allow even a child
any chance of survival.

Last night I dreamed
my German mother among those
outside, speaking in tongues,
in ecstasy to witness
this extermination.
This muse raised her arm.
She screamed.
At ninety-three, she is still screaming.
Her screams made & make
the same sound as the flames.

The Sea

I couldn't see which titles, but they were mine,
boxes of them piled six boxes high, or ten,
or three, the piles tottering, the bottom boxes wet.
I knew my books would suffer, despite their root-

bound overhang, for this was the time of hurricanes,
but I still thought to save them, me with my porous brain,
maybe carry them, or some, maybe at least
a few boxes, a box or two, to higher ground,

so bent my knees properly, but couldn't quite
grip the cardboard to pile a small box onto
a larger one to carry two, then couldn't even rescue one.
Poetry had already slipped into where compost

becomes the sea, that brine oversoul that now
seeped around the boxes & my bare ankles
as I tried to lift armfuls of orphans to my bosom
to awaken where I'd been before I wrote them.

A Note on the Author

William Heyen was born in Brooklyn, New York, in 1940, and raised in Suffolk County by German immigrant parents. His graduate degrees are from Ohio University. A former Senior Fulbright Lecturer in American Literature in Germany, he has been honored with NEA, Guggenheim, American Academy of Arts & Letters and other awards. His *Crazy Horse in Stillness* won the Small Press Book Award in 1997; *Shoah Train: Poems* was a Finalist for the National Book Award in 2004. He is Professor of English/Poet in Residence emeritus at SUNY Brockport.

BOOKS FROM ETRUSCAN PRESS

Legible Heavens | H. L. Hix

Saint Joe's Passion | J. D. Schraffenberger

Drift Ice | Jennifer Atkinson

The Widening | Carol Moldaw

Parallel Lives | Michael Lind

God Bless: A Political/Poetic Discourse | H. L. Hix

Chromatic | H. L. Hix (National Book Award finalist)

The Confessions of Doc Williams & Other Poems | William Heyen

Art into Life | Frederick R. Karl

Shadows of Houses | H. L. Hix

The White Horse: A Colombian Journey | Diane Thiel

Wild and Whirling Words: A Poetic Conversation | H. L. Hix

Shoah Train | William Heyen (National Book Award finalist)

Crow Man | Tom Bailey

As Easy As Lying: Essays on Poetry | H. L. Hix

Cinder | Bruce Bond

Free Concert: New and Selected Poems | Milton Kessler

September 11, 2001: American Writers Respond | William Heyen

etruscan press
www.etruscanpress.org

Etruscan Press books may be ordered from:

Consortium Book Sales and Distribution
800-283-3572
www.cbsd.com

Small Press Distribution
800-869-7553
www.spdbooks.com